LOVE REGULATE LIVE 2nd Part

its therapeutic approach

Dr. Pedro Julio Garcia Linares

SYNOPSIS

It is a book that starts with the author's next question:

What regulates Life since one is born, whether we want it or not?

Its answer is based on the concept of FORCES, which have an objective character, since their manifestations depend on certain structures and functions of the Nervous System.

The weight of each force and its development is determined by the experiences that everyone has had in the historical moment that he had to live.

As for the Force of Love, the Columns that sustain it, become important categories for the analysis of cases with mental disorders, the selection of couples, family conflicts, infidelity and divorce.

Other topics are also addressed in the book, because they touch everyone, in daily life.

Love regulates Life does not pretend to be a textbook, nor does it encompass the wide range that is related to Love.

INTRODUCTION

In the Life of all, Love is a force that participates and regulates the process of formation of many attributes of the Personality concept.

Since we are born, Love participates in our development and determines a lot, what we are after.

Do not doubt that Love is vital to exist, as there are many newborns who have died in orphanages because they did not have the privilege of being caressed by the arms of a mother.

It is a fact, that those who have not had Love in their precise moment, have been upset and their interaction with the World has been distorted.

Love has participated in the Secret War of the old Empires, in the lives of writers, famous artists and many other figures that appear in the annals of History. Love has marked their lives in the multitudes of all times, both men and women.

The secret of why Love is so important for the Human Being, has not been fully clarified by those who have tried to explain so obvious but challenging enigma

Despite its essential role in our becoming as individuals, Love as a subject does not appear in the academic curriculum, nor is it part of teaching in schools.

I think you will agree with me in saying that: "every person deserves to graduate at the University of Life with the best grades in this essential subject". It is rare to meet people who do not need to be loved, who do not mind being part of a family, who do not need good friends and are indifferent to the quality of their human relationships. Feeling alone, not feeling part of the lives of others, makes many unhappy in our days.

The training and education of the human being is usually focused on preparing and programming the individual to be able to work, when on the other hand, the importance of the family in the development of society is emphasized by many institutions. But despite all efforts in this regard by organizations and governments, the number of dysfunctional families in many communities in the world has not stopped growing.

It is no longer news, or anything new, that every year the number of couples who divorce is greater. It has also grown number of children who do not know one of their parents, especially in the early stages of their development. Premature marriages, adolescent pregnancies and domestic violence grow, as the expenses of social services continue to grow in programs that seek to remedy of many factors which regulate the reality Singles clubs and online dating have become fashionable. Television creates programs at the cost of human misery latent in the lives of many families. There are few shows on TV where they beat mother and daughter, wife and husband.

I have wondered if, perhaps because of that, the number and types of religious groups have grown in our times. Men usually groups in search of common ends. Not a few are tired of debauchery. There are not few unbelievers that there is a true, lasting and faithful Love. The more experiences and failed attempts in search of loyalty, understanding and love, the more doubt that there is. There are many and diverse factors associated with this sad reality of our days. Collective impotence has grown and becomes evident when groups of people declare their lack of hope and confidence in the new generations. Love is coming within an antagonistic context, where its charm deteriorates. One of the enemies that fuels this deterioration is the growing struggle for power, drugs and poverty.

There are many who are aware of what has been said, as there are many who are eager to love and be loved.

But they conspire against those expectations, the news and the irrefutable facts of our times. It is not surprising that many ears have been deaf and that the doors of Hope have been closed, for those who have remained skeptical and without response to the facts.

The impotence of the reality that we live reaches some, especially when it cannot be denied that there are children betraying their parents, that there are friends who disappear in the bad and that marriages break more easily. However, this does not crush the optimism of many, who do not lose hope of changing things and that Love is the most important Force in the life of Man.

Newscasts highlight more the negative than the positive that occurs in society. It is a constant poison that disturbs minds. The stories of eternal love, of faithful friends, of children with velvet hearts, who walk among us, without apparently being noticed, are almost never published or ignored.

It is not surprising, that the exceptions increase and the number of people who decide not to try to find a partner for fear of failure has increased.

Impotence and discouragement, depressed and isolated. That's why I think there are not enough books, although there are many. There is a lack of television programs and a cinema, at the service of human welfare. We must defend the right to freedom.

Today innocent deaths are the result of attacks that question whether the human being is capable of love. It is usually done by those who do not accept others, who do not include them, who terrify by taking away the right to feel protected and safe, much less that they can feel loved.

Many have forgotten the holocaust that blinded the lives of millions of people a few decades ago and that had its origin in ideologies that killed the essence of the human being.

There is also, many novels continue to feed the idea that we must protect ourselves from falsehood, from envy and deceit. We are exposed to a bombardment of images that are assimilated, without being properly filtered by our consciousness. This happens sometimes, much more in young people, than in their struggle for the new and their opposition to their predecessors, easily embrace the human miseries that propagate the mass media. Self-centeredness spreads, and the concept of living the present grows, giving it back, to which we are responsible both for our future and for future generations. While, on the one hand, scientists worry about prolonging life and seeking a cure for diseases, others worry about creating weapons of mass extermination.

Love is a necessity inherent in the human condition. Fear has become your worst enemy. The doubt, distrust and fragility that moral values have today, end up encrusting abundant and venous thorns to the most beautiful of flowers.

This delicate Flower, which is the Force of Love, mysteriously obeys other regulators in the history of its development. If your columns are not built during childhood, the course and formation of the Personality can be modified. Which would imply that we would not be what we could be. This, in turn, indicates that the Force of Love is subordinated to a historical determinism. Its bases have a marked hour and a specific way to build. Everything said above reaffirms us, that the weight and strength that Love has in the course of our lives is undeniable. Without ceasing to be less certain, that the Force of Love is vulnerable and fragile. She does not write the whole story herself. The force of Love can be attacked and in turn it can modify the role of other Forces that also mark the course of our existence.

We do not aspire to encompass everything about Love in this book. The intention is to share criteria, knowledge and experience acquired during the course and the exercise of our profession.

ACKOWLEDGMENTS

First, I want to thank all the patients that I have attended throughout my career. Their stories led me to build a therapeutic interpretation approach that I will present in this book.

Secondly, to the pioneers of the psychodynamic approaches of Psychology, which in a certain way have helped me conceptualize that there are Forces that regulate life since one is born.

Thirdly, to my dear wife Maricarmen, for her unconditional support in good times and in bad, as she always tells me. Fourth, my beloved daughters Maydel, Meily and Elena. They are flowers from my garden, which bring a special nectar to my life. Flowers that never wither and that I need a lot. To my beloved son Pedro Pablo because his efforts and dedication to study and sports have filled me with pride and inspired me to move forward. Also, I must mention my sons-in-law, Louis and especially Jorge Gómez, who is not only an example of family love, but also someone who will live within me always, for his unconditional help always.

Fifth, Cove Rincon International, its members and board of directors, for having been the driving force in the Mexico - Miami meeting, of having written the first edition of this book.

Sixth, to the growing development of my spiritual life, in the segment of history in which I am inserted, which has contributed close friends, patients, family and especially Miguel Torres, who with their faith and beliefs have helped to strengthen my life in the moments that I needed it most. Thanks to you, the readers, who will give life to these pages written with Love.

TABLE OF CONTENTS

1- The Forces that Regulate Life.

2- Love can cause physical and mental disorders.

3- Does Love and Sex appear at the same time?

4- Love does not have sex.

5- In search of The Half Orange.

6- Strategies in the choice of the couple.

7- Infidelity.

8- The tragedy of a woman who has been unfaithful.

9- Divorce.

10- Love and menstruation.

11- Should the relationship continue or not?

12- There is not always a second chance.

13- I take my hat off.

1- FORCES THAT REGULATE LIFE.

In possible to find the following classification of the Forces by other authors.

A- Emotional and survival forces (which may also be present in animals) but in man are regulated and determined by thought, social life and the human brain.

B- Psychological forces (exclusive of the man by the participation of the EGO and the formation of the personality)

C- Social forces (learned and internalized during the process of socialization and the formation of the moral (values) in man and the development of personality).

Next, the scheme identifies the Forces that we will describe in the book, which may be included in the classification already mentioned above.

Next, the scheme identifies the Forces that I will describe in the book, which may be included in the classification already mentioned above.

FORCES THAT REGULATE LIFE

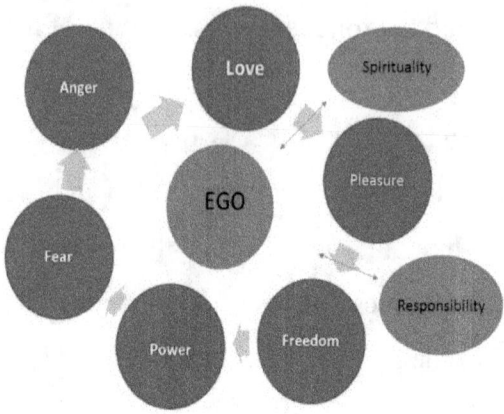

THE STRENGTH OF LOVE.

The central philosophy that is in each great part of this book is since:

"Life is regulated by Forces, some since one is born, whether we want it or not".   PJ.

The development of the Human Brain is characterized by the growth of neural networks and structures of the nervous system that allow us to think and feel in a special way. However, during this development biological and psychological needs are intertwined throughout life, which determine their behavior. Likewise, during the ontogenetic development of the human being, defensive mechanisms and vital needs for survival or conservation appear. Although cognitive-behavioral theories have been able to measure and modify behaviors, it is also true that the behavior of human beings obeys forces that direct their behavior, although they are not easy to measure, with the tools of the current prevailing psychology.

A determining Force that regulates our existence from the moment one is born is Love. Its bases or vertebral columns are acceptance, belonging, security-protection and affection. In the case of couples, it is necessary to include sex. Everything seems to indicate that nature is structured and organized in such a way that all its components are interdependent. That is to say: "Nature does not want totally autonomous or self-sufficient organisms".

The importance of affect in health has been demonstrated by Harvard studies, but never as radically as was the case of the research of Dr. Rene Spitz in the 50s of the twentieth century. The work of pioneer Dr. Rene Spitz was confirmed decades later: babies who grow up without love can die, and most of them grow up with physical and mental illnesses.
(https://pijamasurf.com/2018/03/elestudioquemostro_ quebebesquenorecibenamorcorrenriesgodemorir)
As many cases of adopted children, their lives changed their course of having grown up in a "normal home". We have the case of Steve Jobs, who used drugs, was in

therapy because his mother gave him up for adoption. In my opinion, his ability and his contributions, which led him to be known worldwide, perhaps, had to do to show his mother that he lost the opportunity to raise an exceptional child. Finally, he got to know her.

Scientific research has managed to identify in the Human Brain that structure is activated when we love.

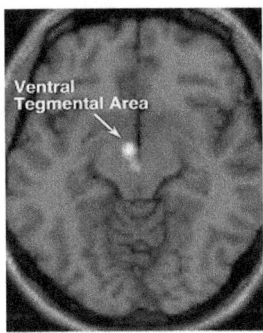

In humans there are four small areas of the brain that, according to some researchers, form the circuit of love. Acevedo, who works at the Albert Einstein College of Medicine in New York, is part of a team that has isolated those regions and given them very unromantic names: ventral tegmental area (ATV), Accumbens nucleus, ventral pale and dorsal nucleus rap ATV is a fundamental component of the brain's reward system.

17

The key element is the ATV. When a person who just fell in love was placed on a magnetic resonance imaging machine and shown photos of their lover, the ATV became enlightened. The same when we observed people who remain deeply in love after 20 years.

The researchers also studied the brains of people who have been married for 20 years and continue holding hands and behaving as if they had just met. In the brains of these men and women, two other areas were illuminated, along with the ATV: the pale ventral and the dorsal raphe nucleus. The pale ventral is associated with affection and hormones that reduce stress, while the raphe nucleus pumps serotonin, which "stimulates a sense of calm," according to Fisher. (https://www.tecomparto.com/te-explicamos-detalladamente-sobre-la-ciencia-del-amor/).

The information previously provided supports the Force of Love is a reality and that it is not a simple term used without theoretical and practical foundation.

Now we will go on to describe how its columns play a role in the development of man's behavior and attitudes.

They are humiliated, physically and mentally abused by others. All this causes that they do not feel accepted. Not only do they not feel accepted, they also do not feel included in the lives of others, they do not feel safe and protected, and much less receive affection from those who mistreat them. As the Force of Love is so important, when its columns are affected, the remaining Forces that regulate Life also break out and react. In most cases we see that Fear grows, as these people lose Power (they subordinate themselves), they lose Freedom (they cannot be as they would like, because they feel harassed and despised). Pleasure becomes displeasure, losing the joy of leaving, of enjoying any event and even some of losing the desire to live. The worst is when the anger increases within these people, because I could lead them to commit acts of violence towards others or towards themselves. We are not unaware of the existence of these dramatic and terrifying cases presented in the news.

The same happens in women victims of domestic violence. Many times, prior to the physical aggression, they had already been mistreated verbally, excessively criticized, having to tolerate insults and infidelities. In the same way the columns of Love were mistreated, and the result is like those who suffer from bullying.

We have had cases in which the personality was modified by the events that occurred during childhood. They have been children who have been raised in the house of uncles or aunts who had children. Their cousins made them feel inferior and intimidated. Many times, uncles or aunts, they made them feel that they did not have the same rights as their children and they turned them into servants of the house, as payment of the roof and food that they were given. Here the Force of Love broke the columns of affection, belonging, acceptance and security. Many became resentful people, with difficulty expressing affection, cranky or, in docile and dependent people. Educators have also unjustifiably used adjectives or qualifiers that have damaged their students and the traces they have left in their minds continue in their lives despite the years. Parents do the same when they become frustrated with the behavior of their children.

We have here the basic elements to try to understand how the relationship between people is affected and how personality traits can impact.

The Forces of Love can also help us to try to repair those affected columns with actions that require persistence and patience.

But it is necessary to understand the rest of the Forces that regulate life, for the analysis of the pending issues to be dealt with in the book.

THE EGO

This psychological structure is unique and exclusive to the human being. Becoming aware of yourself is something possible thanks to the biological development of the Brain and its interaction with the sociocultural moment in which we are inserted. But, because it is so special, it does not appear from the moment we are born. It takes time. Recently, scientists have been able to identify a small part within the frontal portion of the brain, such as the seat of the ego, consciousness and the sense of self. According to them, in the areas called Anterior Cingulate Cortex (ACC) and Fronto-insular Cortex (FIC) is the sense of ego or consciousness. (Neurobiological Basis of Ego and Anger, Anil K. Rajvanshi Nimbkar Agricultural Research Institute).

From the moment babies are born, they are exposed to information that can teach them who they are. By touching your face and body, or kicking and grabbing things, you begin to enjoy the influence of their actions in the world. But it is not until the children approach their second birthday that they begin to develop a sense of self and can reflect on themselves from the perspective of another person. (Josephine Ross, University of Dundee, Douglas Martin, University of Aberdeen, and Sheila Cunningham, University of Abertay).

Research carried out in Kenya made its authors think that the development of self-consciousness is more of a culturally developed skill in a gradual and continuous way, based on the results obtained with the mirror test. Hopkins on the subject of consciousness, says: "Consciousness is like gravity, we cannot touch it directly, so if we want to measure it, scientists must develop valid techniques to directly observe its effects. (http://www.scientificamerican.com/article.cfm?id=kids-and-animals-who-fail-classic-mirror).

The above information allows us to have an idea that the Self and the Self-consciousness is an evolutionary process of the biological development of the Brain and that it takes time to participate in our interaction with the world. This condition can have its drawbacks. I mean that, if some of the columns of the Force of Love have suffered attacks, the situations and emotions experienced, pass to the Unconscious and the infantile EGO that not yet structured, has no way to process what happened in the early ages. This can produce internal conflicts that cause alterations that can be both physical and mental.

The "EGO" is a mediator between the subject and his environment. The EGO interacts with all the Forces that regulate Life through cognitive and emotional processes, in accordance with the level of biological development reached by the nervous system.

This interaction is fundamental in the development of the psychological characteristics of the subject, which will be based on their experiences and the way they use in conflict resolution and how to meet their needs.

Let us use examples to illustrate what has been said previously, since perhaps all the above has a rather technical language.

Let's say, that we can observe at the same time two homes and the mothers or any other relative interacting with your child. Both children (as) are the same age (they can be between 4-5 years old). They are physically healthy, but they are bred differently. Both live in the era of the cult of superheroes. They are wanting their mothers to give them one of those plastic figures of the favorite superhero. It happens that mothers resist this, and children begin to look for a way to be pleased. Let's say that mother A, her son asks for everything, crying. And that mother B, her son asks for it by shouting and showing anger. As you can see, the solution and way to seek the satisfaction of the need is different in both cases, although the reason for their behavior is the same, to obtain a toy. To obtain what they want with these behaviors repeated over time, is supposed to influence the way they are in the future. True?

The way of being accepted and feeling loved has been reinforced differently in each case. That EGO in the future will look in a case, get what you want, perhaps, brave and in the other case, perhaps, react resentful or sad when you do not achieve what you want. For both to be accepted and wanted is obtained in different ways.

There are several defense mechanisms of the SELF facing Life. I recommend looking for this information in the lit That SELF or Ego, of which we could write many pages and we would leave the subject, is subject to genetic determinants and personal experiences. We do not refer to personality styles and personality disorders, which participate in the relationship of parents and couples, of course, impacting the Force of Love.

We also suggest that you look for information in the literature. We do not choose the parents, but we do choose the couple and, often, we do not know their personality. Many times, one of the members of the couple discovers, how is their partner, after a time of being together. Let's say that one of them discovers that his partner begins to show that he is impulsive, that he has frequent mood swings, that he is explosive and with fits of anger and that he has little tolerance for frustration. This brings up arguments and worries, which come to affect the way of giving oneself affection. The security and protection that was felt is in doubt. That is, the columns of Love are shaken and damaged.

How can people who are victims of interacting with such a subject react? There are times when they leave the relationship because of the intoxicating and unpleasant. But there are people who remain in that dysfunctional relationship, hoping that everything will change, but end up subordinated, losing their autonomy, their freedom and suffering the fear of being attacked. That's why it's important to read about personality disorders. We are not born with a book under the arm to raise children or to know how to act in these situations. We must educate ourselves and this is one of the objectives of this book, to provide knowledge that will help us to be happier and able to be the writers of our lives, preventing others from writing it.

THE STRENGTH OF FEAR.

The Fear as Force that regulates Life, also has its representation the Brain.

Again, there is no doubt that we are predestined to feel fear, and this regulates life, whether we want it or not.

The Amygdala is a structure of the Central Nervous System that participates in the storage of memories that are linked by association and, in turn, establishes links with the new emotional events that the person experiences. The Amygdala is a structure underlying the hippocampus. The Amygdala is involved in the processing of emotions, fear and learning. Researchers argue that it plays a role in conditioned fears and fight-and-escape responses linked to the sympathetic. The amygdala determines the meaning of the stimuli, reacting to what happens in the present. This structure has links with the prefrontal area, the limbic system, the temporal lobe, the olfactory system, the hypothalamus, the hippocampus and others, which do not indicate the complexity of their functions and interactions with the external world in Man.

But this can happen in children who are frequently scolded. They come to think and fear that they are not loved, that they are not accepted, especially when they fail to understand the relationship of their behaviors with the attitude of their parents. Others, because parents do not explain the reasons for their punishments or scolding or use a vocabulary full of qualifiers that obscures the possibility that the child may feel loved. This is another example of how the columns of Affection and Acceptance have been affected.

Fear also has its positive side, when it anticipates or avoids the dangers or possible mistakes that we can make.

Many fears are learned, and some do not enslave.

When the tensions in the couple grow, one of the two may experience losing their partner. If the tensions have grown, it is because in the Force of Love, in some of its columns they have suffered some attack. Well because Security has been lost (jealousy, distrust or infidelity) and has even ended affecting the Sex. There may be other reasons, such as, that a member of the couple is not as fond as he was at the beginning, that is, the column of Affection complains and fails to be reciprocated as expected.

But this can happen in children who are frequently scolded. They come to think and fear that they are not loved, that they are not accepted, especially when they fail to understand the relationship of their behaviors with the attitude of their parents. Others, because parents do not explain the reasons for their punishments or scolding or use a vocabulary full of qualifiers that obscures the possibility that the child may feel loved. This is another example of how the columns of Affection and Acceptance have been affected.

Fear also has its positive side, when it anticipates or avoids the dangers or possible mistakes that we can make.

THE FORCE OF PLEASURE

Another great truth is we are predetermined to feel pleasure and that the excesses or defects in this area end up regulating our lives.

The Septal Nucleus is considered as the Center of the Pleasure of the Brain. Dopamine is generally associated with the Pleasure system.

Other authors state that the pleasure center is made up of several brain areas such as the ventral tegmental area, which projects that it projects the connections of its neurons to other areas involved in the process. These areas are: the nucleus Accumbens, the corpus striatum, the anterior cingulate cortex, the hippocampus, the amygdala, and the cerebral cortex. We want to emphasize that the basolateral amygdala is associated with pain and fear and that the nucleus Accumbens is associated with feelings of pleasure and reward.

The important thing is that this Force is also represented in our Brain and its multiple connections tell us how other psychological and emotional processes are linked to pleasure.

31

Emotional tensions cause some people to seek pleasure to alleviate the discomfort produced by these states. Anxiety and depression may be some of them. There are people who calm it down with chocolate, others with cigarettes, or with drugs, alcohol or food. "Looking for pleasure and avoiding pain are the axis of almost all behaviors."

I remember that the grandmothers said that the babies smile in the crib because the angels were interacting with them. Nowadays, we could say that smiling can be an expression of the pleasure they felt while feeding them.

Sex is one of the sources of pleasure of the human being. During sexual activity the thalamus is activated as an inciter. The Brain Amygdala processes desire and behavior. The Hippocampus produces fantasies and memories that facilitate desire. The nucleus Accumbens increases the pleasant activity by means of the production of Dopamine. The Ventral Tegmental Area is activated to produce the orgasm. The hypothalamus facilitates the production of ovules and sperm. The Cerebellum movements during the sexual act.

I think the reader unfamiliar with brain structures will say that, to follow what has been said above about brain structures and their functions in sex, he would have to buy an atlas of the Brain. Would not be bad. I think it would be a good task. The intention is to know how complex the Brain is working so that we feel one of the greatest human pleasures, when in turn it ensures the perpetuation of the species and survival.

Increase culture is not too much. I think these images can help.

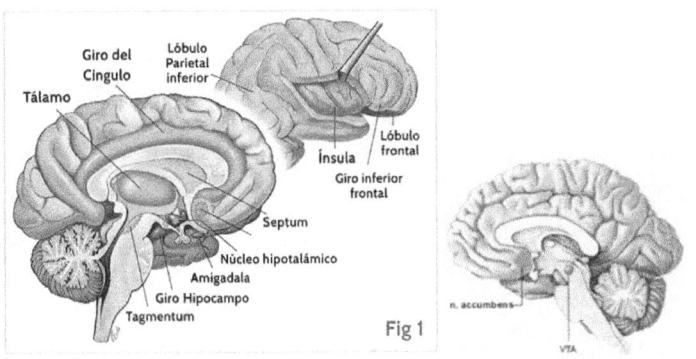

Fig 1

Sex produces pleasure as much as headaches in couples. Women do not always achieve orgasm. They may have a dysfunction due to medical problems, but in many cases the man is responsible. This becomes like a drop after another on top of a rock, which ends up making a hole. Not only is the woman unsatisfied. The man also suffers and gets to wonder if he does not like his wife. What a big problem? The position of how they perform intercourse may be participating. As well as how fast the man reaches orgasm. Not always both are concerned about a previous love game that facilitates that both can be close to the resolution phase.

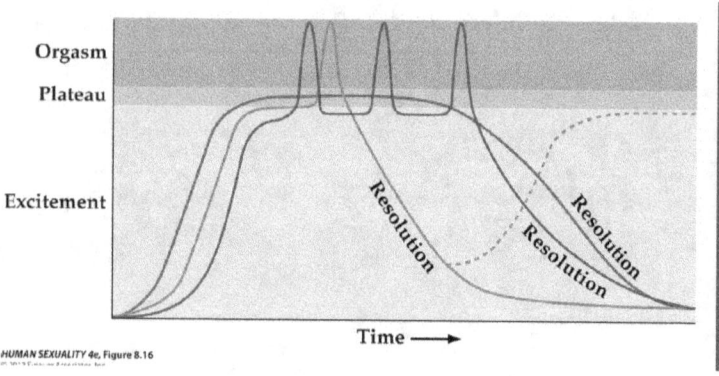

HUMAN SEXUALITY 4e, Figure 8.16

You must find a solution before you complain about the Force of Love and destroy a relationship that started with many illusions. Do not think about it, act on time.

Children feel pleasure playing. It is your main activity for many years. With video games we are witnesses that teenagers, young and not so young enjoy this activity. Do not miss in sports and many recreational activities. On the other hand, depressed people do not feel pleasure in what was previously produced. That it is necessary to feel pleasure there is no doubt. Otherwise, as we have illustrated, the brain would not have the structures and mechanisms to feel it. And to not complicate everything said, we have omitted the role of neurotransmitters in pleasure. But you can also look for information about it. We wonder if it is prudent and necessary that many schools have almost eliminated the time of recess where children can play and thereby reduce the stress produced by the classes. This would not only mobilize pleasurable pleasure mechanisms in the brain but would also facilitate cognitive processes to work more effectively.

This could make the students feel that they want more of their school, interact more with their classmates and increase the sense of belonging, basic column of the Force of Love.

Here is another task for parents in their Community.

THE STRENGTH OF FREEDOM.

At birth, we are put in the cradle. The position adopted is that of supine cubitus (face up). It is not until the first year or a little more that we walk and then we get to run. Parents begin to watch their children walk and we observe that sometimes children do not satisfy themselves and walk away and explore what surrounds them.

Not far with the development of language, children become more demanding. They ask to play with certain friends, or go to the park, etc. In adolescence they want to go alone to the parties to which they are invited. The demands of Freedom are growing.

If we talked about history, we would sit in front of a library full of books that tell us about the wars of nations and peoples in search of their freedom.

Kelsen said: "the more the desire for" power ", the less appreciation for freedom and the greater the probability of authoritarian behavior" (The power and values in Weber, Freud and Kelsen, in the light of the "new scientific paradigm" and in relation to Latin America, Polis Revista Latinoamericana).

everyday life we meet many controlling people who end up being suffocated. Of course, in marriages this abounds on both sides.

Overprotective mothers become people who want everything to control and to which children react, especially in adolescence, lying, escaping from school or home or doing everything contrary to what is expected in their homes.

These situations also affect the Force of Love, in the Security and Protection columns, but not by default but by excess.

THE STRENGTH OF THE ANGER

In the Left Hemisphere, the Temporal Area is linked to violent thoughts and the loss of emotional control related to aggression. In turn, the Pre-Frontal area is considered related to the lack of impulse control. The anterior part of Cingulate Gyrus is where the negative thoughts are parked, and the mind does not find options and outputs. Finally, it is in the limbic system and in the basal nuclei where anxiety and emotional states make theirs, due to an increase in the activity of these brain structures. The limbic structures (amygdala, hippocampal formation, septal area, prefrontal cortex and cingulate gyrus) strongly modulate the aggression through its connections with the medial and lateral hypothalamus. Everything seems to indicate that the basis for feeling anger and aggressiveness is predetermined before birth.

All people get angry sometimes. Sometimes it happens when the person is frustrated for a certain reason. Also, when something goes wrong and your expectations are not met. Between parents and children, it is frequent and in couples too.

The undesirable of these situations is that words are said to be offensive or adjectives that last in memories sometimes throughout life. When it happens, the Force of Love is sometimes affected in several of its columns, according to the case.

Aggression can have its charms when without being violent or doing harm, it frees us from a dangerous situation.

THE STRENGTH OF RESPONSIBILITY

Nobody is born responsible. During ontogenesis, multiple factors contribute to being consistent and responsible. Education is an important factor that may be interfered with and blocked the sense of responsibility for certain brain conditions. It cannot be generalized, but parents who have children with ADHD (attention disorder with hyperactivity) complain that they leave homework to do, however much they are reminded to do their homework with the school). The so-called psychopaths are not responsible at all with society or with the family and, there are studies of the brain that indicate that they have certain dysfunctions in the Brain.

The personal sense of responsibility is marked by much, by the values of the person, family and society. The sacrifices of the mothers are true examples of this affirmation. As are the heroic acts of men who shine in history.

41

THE STRENGTH OF EXPERTUALITY.

It is not strange that man has always sought spirituality as a method to give a logical explanation to the things that happen in the world and his life.

There are those who consider that what we call spirituality are experiences in which certain structures of our brain, which are very active. In some cases, these experiences have been called altered states of consciousness, and in these states the subject presumably meets supposed spiritual beings.

There are studies, related to temporal epilepsy, relationship with the spiritual life and with well-known personalities in history. Among them are: Saul of Tarsus, Mohammed, Joan of Arc, Saint Catherine of Genoa, Saint Catherine of Ricci, Saint Teresa of Lisieux, Joseph Smith, founder of the Church of Jesus Christ of Latter Day Saints, that is to say of the religion of the Mormons, who also suffered from epilepsy. Others with the same brain disorders are Dostoevsky, Vincent van Gogh or Emanuel Swedenborg and many others.

The question that arises is when the human being began to have spiritual experiences. In the Middle Paleolithic (between 130,000 and 33,000 BC) and in the Upper Paleolithic (between 33,000- and 9,000-years BC) graves have been found in which are the bodies of the deceased accompanied by tools and hunting implements, which points to the belief in a life beyond death. The American neurologist Kevin Nelson, in his book The Spiritual Doorway (The Spiritual Entry in the Brain), says the following: "The mystical is not beyond language in a neurological sense. It is before language, residing in archaic brain structures that have to do with our Darwinian survival.

Since the brain is known to produce spirituality, two possibilities are posed: the position of believers that can argue that God has placed structures in the human brain that allow spiritual experience and contact with the divine and that which sets forth spiritual experiences are fruitful of evolution, like the rest of the organism, that is, by the process of natural selection, which would lead us to wonder what survival value these structures would have.

If the structures are the fruit of evolution, which seems obvious, there is still the possibility that a divine design has made it possible using the mechanisms of evolution to reach man and that it was this that could have the spiritual and spiritual experiences. That way we can communicate with spiritual beings. But the opposite position is also possible, namely that these structures are what have generated the beliefs in spiritual beings as an accessory product of other functions linked to the emotional brain. (https://www.tendencias21.net/La-espiritualidad-humana-tiene-su-origen-en-estructuras-cerebrales_a17073.html). This package of ideas leads us to realize the complexity of the topic and what remains to be clarified by the researchers.

The truth is that the belief in something higher is present in previous and present generations without reaching to be universal, because there are also those who do not believe in God or spiritual things. However, the spiritual part participates in many people in a positive way when it is linked to Hope, Peace and Protection. Likewise, it can be negative, when it is obsessive or has an excessive role in feelings of guilt.

There is the case of those who had beliefs in God or something higher but lose it when a loved one dies in an accident or when a child dies due to medical negligence or unexpectedly.

2-LOVE CAN CAUSE DISORDERS PHYSICAL AND MENTAL

The Story of (Dora)

Many years of happiness characterized their marriage relationship. The joy of feeling respected, loved and cared for rushed the day her husband fell ill. The abrupt change of economic life and losing the independence they enjoyed began to grind their lives. The situation worsens when the medical treatment received by the husband, produces a sudden change in personality. Now, that attentive, flattering and loving husband has become a jealous man, distrustful in the extreme, who accuses her of being unfaithful and of pretending to other men. By making his mind sick, his mind became dirty and destroy with his thoughts and actions, the charm of a special love story. Depression begins to gnaw at Dora. The reason for this depression is the impotence that triggers the feelings that it is not possible to change the things. She feels threatened and unhappy. She is no longer to be accepted, protected and flattered wife. Love stopped being fed in the usual way.

Now, he suffers from arthritis, fibromyalgia, high blood pressure and nodules in the toroid. The significance of the story is that before she was a healthy person.

The History of Maya.

Since she was born, life condemned her to be a rejected person. Her mother refused to look like her father, saying she was ugly and fat every day. I leave her to the grandmother's care to dedicate herself to an unscrupulous sex life.

At 14 years old, she gets married, maybe to get out of his first hell.

It did not take many years for their marriage to end in a divorce. Their new relationship was even more humiliating. She is now married to a womanizing man, who also called her ugly. The emotional abuse to which he subjected her was such, that she allowed him to walk with other women in her own neighborhood. All this accentuated her low self-esteem. Maria begins to suffer from depression and a strong arthritis that begins to prevent her from working.

A little over two years ago, her husband dies of a bullet in the head, for maintaining relations with a married woman. The husband of that woman is the one who supposedly as The Love that she never received, made her a slave to feel the need to belong to someone. The permanent rejection made her sick and made her a dependent woman.

The hope that one day, her husband would repent and recognize the unconditional love that she professed, makes her believe that the spirit of her husband is around her and because of that, she spends time talking to him in her imagination and even feels that he responds many ways.

The Story of Clara.

This young woman grew up in a home dominated by the Christian faith. His mother's expectations were that he would comply with all the rules of the religion. One of this rule stays that you could not have sex until the marriage was consummated. But she fell in love and had sex, ending, knowing the mother.

Clara's depressed mood already had her background in her relationship with her father and her isolation, caused by the control and overprotection of both parents.

She had to be helped to process her traumatic experiences at school by teasing and harassment.

Clara was hospitalized due to her depression and because she was hurting herself with suicidal attempt due her parents did not give her the affection she needed, but they later changed after she was admitted to the hospital.

She believes that she has lost the best years of her adolescence in her home because her parents do not allow her to do anything.

Clara maintained low self-esteem in terms of her physical appearance. Anxiety was part of his daily life.

Clara maintained a behavior characterized by a face without emotional expressions, without showing any type of affective type, as if feelings had frozen, after hospital admission.

Her thinking was fixed and repetitive, saying that her body felt nothing. Her mind filled with feelings of guilt because he had not been faithful to the faith and expectations of her family. All this led her to develop a defense mechanism characterized by anesthetizing any response of her body that was related to sex (this reminds conversion hysteria (it is a conversion because the patient converts the psychological conflict into a physical disorder, with anesthesia and sensory losses) And maybe, with a dissociative state, when you wanted to hurt yourself.

The Force of Love participates in their reactions, when the Acceptance, Belonging and Affection column were mistreated by the expectations of the home and her low self-esteem.

The History of Christopher

Cristóbal goes to a mental health center looking for help. During the interview, he says that he feels very nervous, sad and has difficulty falling asleep. He adds that his thoughts do not let him rest. He lets us know that he knows that his wife has asked for a divorce, due to his bad character and frequent arguments. This has characterized their marriage for years. Cristóbal is aware that his behavior at home has also affected his daughter, so he feels guilty.

What is told is enough to realize that the Force of Love has made Christopher need help. His behavior broke the columns of Love. Now, he does not feel accepted because he is not allowed to belong to the family he created. The affection he received and the feeling of being protected by being part of a family nucleus are over.

Did he look for it? Everything seems to indicate that it was. Not only did he argue and become verbally violent, he also abused alcohol for a while, and this helped his bad behavior. The roots of the problem are in Cristóbal's progenitors. His mother abandoned Cristóbal's father because of his verbal abuse. Cristóbal grew up without the maternal heat and it hurt him to realize that all his friends grew up with his parents, except him.

Cristóbal could not give his wife what he did not have inside, because he did not know it during his childhood. He grew up without knowing how to give and receive Love. This indicates to us, that we are in a large part, that in which we have trained ourselves. If you do not drive an airplane, it's because you're not trained. If you do not know how to swim, it's because you're not trained.

This other story reaffirms us, the importance of knowing the family history of who we are in love with. The importance of forecasting the future of our relationship in time.

This story invites us to think that we should all learn more about Love, either to prevent our lives from having such bitter gulps or, to seek help and modify the previously existing conditions in our lives, so that they do not lead us to failure.

The Story of Juan José

Juan José arrives tormented at the psychotherapy office. He was very restless while depressed. Exposing their problems showed their difficulties in making decisions. He had been a successful man in sports and business. Happy to have an excellent wife, with whom he had two children.

However, he confessed to having a history of infidelities. Over time, it is discovered that his wife was never passionate, nor filled him with the tenderness that Juan José needed, despite his constant requests and complaints.

He was dissatisfied, but stuck in a stable home, accompanied by an understandable, honest, faithful and good mother. These premises facilitated an extramarital relationship, but in which he was trapped, because he found what he did not have in his home and more.

Juan José met a girl much younger than him, beautiful, passionate and affectionate. He found someone, as he never had, as he thinks. It begins like this, the history of conflicts, which emotionally mismatch him and make him ask for help.

But although, the unsatisfied Love is the premise of its history, the Fear is the one that predominates in its attitudes and its failure.

Juan José is characterized by being impulsive and regulated by family values, which make him feel guilty in this situation. He did not want to be criticized by his family and his wife's.

But he could not be right with God and the Devil at the same time. However, he began to leave his wife's home on multiple occasions, eventually returning because remorse did not leave him alone.

He did not anticipate the damage he was causing to his young and new partner, who had to tolerate that he was sharing Juan José from time to time with his wife, without being able to determine what place she really occupied in her life.

The discussions and the thorns grew. The girl's family began to censor her, telling her that she was blind and playing an unworthy role with a much older man.

The prognosis was evident. The antagonistic contradictions would put an end to a story of Love that may never be repeated in the life of Juan José. What we are sure is going to repeat and knock on his door, are the unmet needs for affection and attention that he did not know in his marriage and if, in another person.

3- DOES LOVE AND SEX APPEAR AT THE TIME?

We could start by saying that Love and Sex do not appear simultaneously in life. That Love and Sex are regulators of behavior that respond to different biological, social, spiritual and psychological aspects of the human being. This does not deny that Love and Sex interact and can be conditioned with each other in a very special way.

Sex plays a fundamental role in the reproduction of both animals and man. That is, sex allows us to perpetuate as a species.

Many generations were required that in order to have sex they had to love first. How many pairs were marked by this precondition?

How many women were forced into marriage for convenience, without knowing what Love was. And I think, it still happens.

Sex is a biological regulator that is demanding. In how many difficulties have many people been seen by their demands? How many have it cost them to be unhappy, much of their lives, for not having felt sexually satisfied with their partner?

A good question before continuing, at what age does sexual pleasure appear in life?

Although many find it difficult to accept it, sexual desire appears from we are little, from childhood. It is enough for a child to discover the pleasure areas on his own or that unfortunately someone will stimulate these areas, so that life changes them. The news is responsible for reporting these abuses, because unlike a few years ago, families now watch more for the mental health of their children, than for what others could say. In other times, families hid these facts.

Many teenage boys take more time than necessary in the shower and I suppose you can imagine why. The biological demands ask to be satisfied in many cases before love is known. Although it is no less true, there are stories of schoolchildren, in love with their teachers or neighbors. But again, in none of the illustrated cases, love and sex appear at the same time. There are always exceptions, because generalizing is not always prudent, nor wise. We have briefly reviewed things of daily life that we all know.

The important thing is that we keep in mind that Sex and Love do not always go together.

For Love, there are women who have sacrificed their sex life, just as there are men who have sought sex outside the home for not being satisfied with their wife, when they continue to love her.

Many times, these men do not want the lovers as companions of their lives, nor do they want to destroy the home they have formed. These stories are not exclusive to the male sex. There are stories in all parts of the world, where there are women who have been sexually infidels. The question is whether, when women have sex with another man, they do it only for pleasure or they also have a compromised heart.

Years ago, I read a book called "Endocrinological Psychiatry" written in the 50's. A fundamental part of this book was centered on the search for endocrine determinants that gave an explanation to homosexuality. The methods and means used at that time failed to answer the scientific question.

In the 80s, I personally met Dr. Siefried Schanb, who was an authority on Sex in Germany, in those times. In his book "Man and Woman in Intimacy", published in 1978, he dedicates a chapter to the theme of Homosexuality. In this chapter Dr. Schanb writes: "In addition, among homosexuals authentic love can also occur".

Dr. Schanb clarifies that we must avoid classifying someone as a homosexual because they have occasionally had sexual contacts with other people of the same sex. Recognizes that there are bisexual people, who are those who seek in a woman or man, the function of erotic and sexual partner.

According to his research is considered that the homosexual is a very sensitive person, who are easily offended, irritable, unbalanced, easy to influence, nervously unstable and even neurotic. In my opinion, the writing by Dr. Schanb is a generalization.

The homosexual condition does not make everyone equal psychologically.

If we have found in psychotherapeutic practice, that homosexuals, fall in love, they get jealous, they have problems with the couple and that a large percentage of them, achieve labor and cultural success.

We cannot deny that they have been discriminated, not understood, by different cultures, religions and governments. Of that I think that there is no doubt, it is in history.

Interpretations and explanations given to homosexuality, at different times by religions and medicine, have perhaps been the key to their rejection and marginalization. As well as, the fear of "infecting others with their condition", that is, turning them into homosexuals, may also have been part of the attitude of rejection of homosexuality.

No less important in the non-acceptance of these persons, it has been the behavior of some homosexuals in social life. I want to clarify before continuing, that the observations I have done and that are published here, they are facts that can be validated in television programs and public life. The excessive femininity expressed in gestures, movements, double meaning and the wardrobe that adapts to some homosexuals, is not always well received, although it is funny for some. There are many people, who have not applauded. We should understand and accept the opinions and tastes of other people.

I just wanted to point out that in the History of Humanity there is enough evidence that love does not have sex. Heterosexuals fall in love like homosexuals.

5- LOOKING FOR HALF OF OUR ORANGE.

Many of us ask ourselves where? And how? Find our orange half. No less frequent is asking us, if in truth there is that other person somewhere in this world, that comes to our complement, that we need to feel that we find, the other half of our life. In most cases, the answer is yes. Of course, it exists! What usually happens is that we do not know how to do the search.

Mistrust and uncertainty stand in the way and end up being the biggest obstacle to achieving the realization of such an important desire. Above all, as time goes by and our previous experiences have not been good.

For young people it is something different to start after a failure.

Various factors can conspire against the realization of this beautiful dream. We are prisoners of history in the first place. Sometimes we are not geographically in the right place. Others, our economic conditions do not provide us with the necessary freedom. We make hasty decisions, then we regret the failures.

This happens many times, because we have not been trained or educated about Love in a careful way. We jump from children to young people without the appropriate resources to face the demands of that force that regulates our lives so much.

The need to love and be loved is sometimes imperative. In other cases, the search to mate with someone is sought as an exit or escape.

After all, it is like facing the scourge of a storm, without the essential means to avoid disasters. The love of parents is no longer enough. We want to join another person and experience the shaking of a kiss and those other emotions that shake our chest.

The comments and experiences of others on the subject increase our curiosity. The scenes seen in the cinema and television increase our impatience. Internal demands do not know how to wait. Hormones accelerate the process.

The need to share with someone and to feel, is taking over our thinking.

When we are young, we feel distracted, more concerned about the account to meet with friends and to go out.

Sometimes, it happens that even studies are not the priority of the day.

At present, this does not happen to everyone, but those who feel in love, argue that it has happened to them like that. As Love is impetuous and demanding, it can lead us down wrong paths.

Therefore, we have illustrated in the previous paragraphs, things that happen in real life. It is also part of real life, the growth of marriages and premature pregnancies, born of the passion without brakes, of Love in youth.

As calm comes after the storm, it happens that many times the lovebirds separate. At the end of their shocks, there is no doubt that there is not one for the other. New attempts to give and receive love occur. But if the attempts are unsuccessful, the theme of the twin souls knocks on the door.

In our chest you can listen to that inner dialogue in which the questions that anguish our existence. Each question, however different it may be, bears doubts on its back, on whether we can find that other half that we lack, the true companion of life.

If we are the ones who already have children, the matter becomes more difficult. We can no longer think only of ourselves. We are afraid that someone could harm our children. We are terrified that our children will not be accepted.

We are anguished, that tomorrow we should to curse the day we submitted them to share the love and attention they expected, with a stranger. Sometimes it goes well, but in many cases the experience is not what you would have liked to have. The selection process used plays an important role, as well as the principles and the moral code of the couple.

We have assisted many people suffering from depression and within them, women whose depression has worsened because after several marriages, they still feel lonely and lack love. Worst of all, the failures make them suffer from a fear of not finding the person who will fill her with joy and love.

No less dramatic have been the experiences of children whose mothers suffered from psychiatric disorders. These children were trapped in childhood experiences. These traumas, not being overcome, ended up alienating the way they sought love.

Let's cite the case, of those people who had a distant mother and full of anger, whose relationship did not facilitate a hug, nor the simplest and most common love words (I love you my son / daughter!), You are special in my life! , How much I need you !, how proud I am to have you !, etc.).

The absence of these words in the lives of these people ends up leaving marked the desire to receive words of love and affection. However, with the passing of the years, nothing changed, not even when their mothers grew old. The innocent of these people waits, but did not mature despite the years, because they never came to see, they could not expect from a sick mother, the behavior of a healthy person.

What they expected bordered on the irrational. What they were looking for exists and maybe, they could watch it in the movies or in another home, but not in theirs.

But these people cannot understand that: "tree that is born crooked, never its trunk straightens" There are those who are not going to change. Then, it is wasting time.

I insist on the importance of knowing certain details of the family life of the person attracts us and in what we think could be our partner. A good forecast can prevent disasters from bad weather.

How to find that person among so many people that I do not even know? Skip the fear. Let your heart feel and do not demand that you reason. But it is important that you consider, everything is recommended below.

6- STRATEGIES IN THE ELECTION OF THE COUPLE.

1- What usually leads to the success of the relationship, is to start after both have realized that they like, they are attracted, that is, that there is what is popularly called chemistry.

A relationship should not be initiated by recommendations or because the person is or looks good.

2- Feeling good in intimate life, in sexual life is very important. It varies with age and with previous experiences. This is a reality that many find it hard to accept. Maybe that's why men emphasize this aspect from the beginning. "It is very popular to listen, "if in the privacy it works, everything else is worth it. "

3- Many people are not clear about what they are really looking for in a new relationship. It is recommended that each one get to know in detail what they need and what they expect from their partner (take time to think about it and write it down). It is also important that you be aware of the things that, if you miss the relationship, could mistreat it over time.

Sometimes, on their own, we do not know how to get that knowledge, and that is when it is advisable to have previously visited a professional who will help us in this search process. It can happen that a previous relationship has marked us. Many people continue to drag the past into their present life and produce expectations and attitudes that interfere with the process of starting over.

4-Many people do not know how to ask themselves the precise questions to make their decisions. They do not know how to study or explore the life of their potential partner, in order to know, if it is real as shown or it is so, because they want to provide the best image during the process of conquest.

5-Many people do not know enough or do not take into account, as their defects and virtues will participate in the dynamics that are established in a couple. Nor do they know about their abilities to adapt to the change that a daily relationship produces as it is in a marriage.

Many people say, "I am like that. Whoever wants to buy me and who does not sell me. " But a couple is a problem of two. A couple usually emerges from the interaction of two strangers who may come to love each other so much, that one without the other, they do not know how to live. Now, this usually happens when both live to make each other happy.

That is why it is important to identify:

a) What does my partner need to be happy?

b) Can I provide what my partner needs, without it costing me a lot of effort?

n the previous example, which is real life, it is palpable one of the many Antagonistic Contradictions, which puts an end to the system of relationships between two people.

6- Many people put so many conditions to accept someone, that they end up sabotaging what they want to achieve. An analysis of those conditions is important.

In the previous example, which is real life, it is palpable one of the many Antagonistic Contradictions, which puts an end to the system of relationships between two people.

6- Many people put so many conditions to accept someone, that they end up sabotaging what they want to achieve. An analysis of those conditions is important. You've to write them on paper and review them a few days later. Then an order of priorities must be established. Say which are those that are not negotiable, because they are linked to our fundamental needs and which needs are the product of always wanting one the best.

It is important not to ignore expectations and needs, whether yes or not, it is a reflection related to our insecurities and beyond what is necessary for the couple to function properly. We cannot forget that fears write many pages of our lives.

We repeat and affirm that in love there are no recipes. Each relationship of love between two people is unique in all its magnitude.

7- THE INFIDELITY

Do you think that the traces left by infidelity make it difficult to return to love?

There are no easy answers to deal with difficult issues. Many will say that it is not possible to feel and act as before, after having been betrayed or deceived.

Infidelity can be conditioned or related to many factors. Generally, we do not expect to be betrayed. At least, that's how we want it to be.

We do not accept the physical or emotional connection of our partner with another person. All that is condemned and sensitive in many cultures. If I remember correctly, in the past, Eskimos generously gave their wives to visitors or guests. What do you think? Without scruples, remorse, jealousy or any other of those feelings that wake up, when we know or think that our partner has done it.

Just as we do not "wait" to get sick, or that we are going to die, or that we are going to lose our social or economic position, or that a very close relative dies, we are not prepared for infidelity.

When it happens, we feel that the other person is dirty, that it is difficult to touch or intimidate her or him again, and we are terrified of what others may think, if we make the decision to accept it and return to the person.

The pain is so great that it disturbs our sleep, our desire to eat, our state of mind and our ability to do daily life. All this takes place, because of the personal meaning that this event has. Excuse me for repeating it, but we are not prepared to face a life event, which stands out for its high emotional load and which nevertheless happens very frequently nowadays.

Without wanting to get away from the subject, I would like to comment on some things in the history of certain civilizations that could help us in the analysis of factors linked to infidelity.

It is not unknown to us that prostitution exists and is practiced.

The sexual fantasies and demands of certain men have been satisfied for a long time with prostitutes. Wives were not supposed to do certain things in privacy at other times due to certain religious beliefs. Not all wives are willing to have intimacy every day.

Arabs have had harem for centuries. The Cesar of the Romans had certain privileges that allowed him orgies and more than one relationship.

It is not new, that sex is a demand for pleasure that does not always sleep in the arms of love.

But infidelity is not always caused by erotic desire. Many women become unfaithful because of the need for attention, affection and good treatment, for a long time absent. Then, of course, that sex seals the passion that springs from the feeling nourished by someone who has known how to fill it with happiness.

Those who know themselves as loved and respected are happy. Those people who are not respected and loved, they lack affection, they do not know what is the word "I love you", nor know the unexpected details of their partner, nor the request in bed, nor the daily compliments and much less that someone is present when their partner needs it, they cannot be happy and have a satisfied love.

All those ingredients make the person who provides them, be a special person in the life of the other. That is why the other person is needed. When you love, your partner is needed.

If we can continue or make our life, without feeling a vacuum when our partner is absent, without missing him or her, without needing to see him or her, without needing to be close to him or her, without the desire to possess your partner don't make your to feel suffocate, what we feel, it could happen that it is not real love. Because, "I like you" it is not the same that "I love you".

But beware! Because love matures and does not demand the same from everyone.

When the binomial love and sex, has broken and both walk separately, we demand a solution. We will deal with it later.

8-THE TRAGEDY OF A WOMAN WHO HAS BEEN UNFAITHFUL.

Infidelity is part of history even of great characters. Let's review the case of a woman dedicated to her family, who began to be unfaithful to her husband. Perhaps, feeling alone in a union of many years and the fear of aging without tasting the honey that produces the enjoyment of an adventure, led to infidelity.

Let's review the case of a woman dedicated to her family, who began to be unfaithful to her husband. Perhaps, feeling alone in a union of many years and the fear of aging without tasting the honey that produces the enjoyment of an adventure, led to infidelity. The little enjoyment she had does not alleviate the pain she now suffers. Pain and guilt cover her daily life, together with the uncertainty of whether what she did could remain in the past and in oblivion.

There is no doubt that many times we are deaf to the complaints of our partner, children or friends. Unmet needs are expressed through complaints. For example: "you are not as affectionate as before", "you just spend time and pending your children and do not look for a time for me", "the damn computer is first that me", "we never go alone to the movies", etc. .

These complaints or observations must be taken in consideration, because it indicates dissatisfaction with what, if satisfied, would make the other person happy. If one member of the couple complains, it is because he is not happy with what is happening. Its importance cannot be minimized. No, that would be a serious mistake.

Many people come together without fully knowing their partner's past life. There are needs acquired during life that will regulate what we thought and what we are capable of doing.

There are people who, if they do not receive certain attention, feel lonely. Others are very demanding of affection. Many times, the other member of the couple dismisses this and they believe that they are giving everything, when their partner does not think it or feel it that way.

We've to be aware of the details. Which applies to our children too. But who says the children, applies to other relatives. We live prioritizing everything related to the material (work, household items, etc.). But that is worth so much effort, if as a result, it happens that all members of the household are dissatisfied with us, because they have not felt served as expected.

It does not mean that you've to live pending just to make others happy. But if we are going to go through life without leaving roots, we have neglected important things. The price that is paid is that we will quickly go into oblivion.

If we focus on the case at hand, carelessness has caused the other person is no longer necessary in her life. She already doubts whether she loves or not, she doubts if it is worthwhile to follow the relationship of many years in which her husband has not made changes and probably will not be now or ever. Much more, after the distrust that produces an adultery.

The dissatisfied person will seek different arguments to justify that it is not worthwhile to follow a false and the rest of his or her life without feeling fully, although perhaps she or he does not find what she or he wants.

No one knows what He has, until He loses it.

9- THE DIVORCE

The divorced woman increases in many places nowadays. Unlike in other times, the culture of the divorced woman has changed in certain countries. The woman does not feel the same stigma of being a divorced woman and with the same intensity as in the past. A few decades ago, it was a family and personal problem. Being divorced, could mark the woman for the rest of her days.

Not being a virgin to get married again, it made her feel different and not equal in virtue. The doubt of being accepted or loved by another man had other dimensions. If she had children, the situation could make her feel worse and with less hope. Maybe, women did not stop having those who wanted them, but the doubt of good intentions, built a barrier difficult to overcome.

The woman has not stopped suffering for many generations. The machismo or egocentrism of man, culturally approved for centuries, has disadvantaged them, above all, in all the times in which women have depended economically on their conjugate.

To the extent that women have inserted themselves into economic life and have conquered their own income, things have changed. Which does not mean that there are still many women, who begin in the marriage career without anticipating that they need economic independence, if they want to ensure they suffer less, in case of that they are separated or divorced. The illusion of love and the lack of adequate preparation for such an important career, does not let them anticipate the future that awaits them.

It must be considered that many women come from homes where mothers have not been the best example for their descendants to make their life different. The descendants repeat the same stories and the chain of broken families continues its course.

No less true, that when a woman commits herself to marriage, she neglects her old friendships. If their marriage is destroyed, they no longer have a contemporary support group. In any of the cases, they can find in some family member support to continue their life.

Since they do not conceive of going out alone to certain places, it is more difficult for them to think about where to get a couple or where to have a good time. If the separation was unexpected and I was still in love, it is harder to think of another man. If you have children, the fear that another man may be around your children becomes a challenge filled with mistrust.

In addition, many children resist to see their mother in the arms of another man and is not uncommon, to oppose a stranger to put authority and rules in their home. Follow the woman in disadvantage and against, with all the daily responsibilities on her shoulders.

If it was the woman who decided to end the relationship, due to abuse or incompatibility of characters, her heart may be more open to accept another man in her life. But, even so, the stages through which the one who divorces happens, are inevitable. Some consider the stages of divorce similar to those that have a family loss. But we differ in such similarity, because their differences do not cease to exist. The impotence of being able to change reality is in both cases a common psychological factor. Only, in the case of divorce is not absolute lack of hope, in every way. A bit, because you can still think about recovering the marriage or because you can think about starting a new relationship at any time.

When someone dies, this is not possible. So, we think that the categories of Impotence and Lack of Hope responsible for Depressive states in those who have had a loss are not regulated in the same way in divorces. It is added a specific filter in the case of divorces. It is a filter that opens doors to outputs that lead to new solutions. The loss of a relative seems to be a dead end, because it is not reversible to have what no longer exists. In both cases, the defensive mechanisms are activated, and the compensation mechanism can be one of the most frequent.

There is a radical, obvious and objective difference between the loss of a family member and the loss due to divorce. In the loss by divorce, what is missed and strange still exists, has not disappeared. Therefore, the lack of hope is not absolute but relative, as is the feeling of impotence. The acceptance of a divorce may take a long or short time, but it is reached because we are not waiting for life to return the impossible.

On the contrary, it is based on thinking that what has been lost and what one wants to have depends on Self. Of course, you do not get to think that way overnight. Getting to think like that takes time. The one who suffers the most in a separation is the one who has depended the most on the other. Loving is also needing another.

To stop needing someone who loves and who goes against our true desires is not easy. When it is achieved, it is because the dependency has stopped enslaving us and we begin to give ourselves a new opportunity.

There is no doubt that the loss of a child is not the same as the loss of the spouse at a certain age and after many years of happy marriage, to the pain caused by the loss of a sick mother, which was already expected his departure. We cite these cases, to point out that the Personal Meaning of each life event is a psychological variable that regulates the impact of everything that happens to us. If we want to make an objective interpretation of the changes and how they affect us, we've to measure in some way, the individual significance of what happened.

What is the meaning of breaking marriage and home for us? It is very individual, but for most it is not easy. There are not a few men who, after they have left, want to return. As the saying goes: "nobody knows what he has until he loses it". The risky thing is, that sometimes they realize late. Love is delicate and sensitive.

It may not have completely extinguished its fire, but perhaps, no longer the same wood that fed it. Firewood is consumed with dislikes and fights. Separations, even if followed by reconciliations, do not cease to lacerate feelings. The intention to start over and give each other another chance does not eliminate the doubts and the wounds that have been passed by magic.

At some point the flames of disgust are fanned. If this happens, this may be an indicator that the causes of marital conflicts were not treated very well. It can be thought that the push for reconciliation was provoked by old feelings or by the consequences that the breakup of the home might have for the children.

There are those who affirm that in the minds of those who are separated, there is a fear of losing what they were used to. How to distinguish if what unites us now is by Love or is the habit? These questions are not missing. Nor are there those who say that after a reconciliation, marriage is not the same. What is what is no longer the same? What explains the change?

Are we talking about what someone had? Are we talking about what was neglected? Are we talking about what was expected to be marriage? Are we referring to questioning if we really get married in love? Are we referring to the fact that the wounds do not cease to anguish us and do not give peace to our thoughts? Are we talking about the difficulty of knowing how to forgive?

We better stop, because the questions would not stop. We leave to you the questions that I have not asked. There is not always an answer for everything. Everything that is felt during this process, often lacks words that explain it. What, if it is clear, that for many it is no longer the same.

Who says that it is not the fear that is playing its role now? Divorce, fights and dislikes hurt Love. Like it or not, experiences are part of the mud that shapes our expectations.

Emotional pain is a lap of thorns that we all try to avoid making us bleed. If it were a delicacy, it is not a delicacy that we like to repeat.

Even in a reconciliation, deaf ears follow the requests or complaints that come from who is next to us. Being that way, how to know that the problems will not be repeated? We calm the uncertainty and the fear of separation by being together again, but we do not give answers to what daily exhausts and disappoints us. The change, where is the change? The screams of the dissatisfied soul are felt after a short time and these produce crises in the couple, one after the other. The tolerance to the crises becomes the arguable point that triggers the rupture at any time again. The discouragement, the sadness and the bad sleep appear, and they denounce that they are suffering. Irritability and anger declare war on welfare and harmony. Everyone in the home is contaminated and the toxins of unhappiness leave their mark on the faces and chest of the protagonists. Distance and silence are used as shields to avoid being wounded again in daily coexistence. Loneliness becomes the shadow that leaves the next morning without light. The days seem winter, plumb and gray. The coldness is felt in the stomach, where a terrifying void is felt. The look withers and strays, to the point that the eyes stop perceiving the beautiful and the heart the joy. This is a good time to repeat one of my thoughts, "Problems not solved in time, end up making us sick".

The disease gives way when the reproaches are avoided and the constant repetition of everything that has hurt us. There is no wound that heals if we continue to open it. It takes will and desires to love and be loved so that magic can occur. This remedy does not exist in any pharmacy. Laments are not good counselors either. How to be responsible and consistent with our needs and feelings? What do we do with the pride that stands so much in the way?

The foundations on which the relationship rests are the pillars that determine the resistance of these storms. Basic elements of these foundations are: the intensity of the sense, the unforgettable and indestructible moments, the attention never received, the passion in privacy, the dreams woven together, the experiences we acquired in our parents' home and then transferred to the home that we decided to create, the values learned and our character.

Many couples do not have a good foundation. Well, because from the beginning you did not spend enough time to create a story that had the basic elements to need each other or because the character or personality were not complementary. It is unfortunate to realize late. The troubles of passion help make mistakes.

Will we be on time?

10- LOVE AND MENSTRUATION.

Maybe, the title will have awakened curiosity. But do not be surprised that it makes sense when you start reading. When we stopped to think about all the biological aspects that are linked to reproduction and sex, we realized that the preparation of the female organism for fertilization has implications for the intimacy of the couple. I started to laugh, when I commented to someone, that perhaps the Arabs had a Harem for that reason. Thus, this natural phenomenon would not stop them in sexual relationships, because there would be a choice. It's a joke! We do not wish to offend anyone, nor is it our intention that men begin to use this observation to justify their adventures. It's just to give a little humor to the subject.

Going back to the subject with seriousness, menstruation, "sometimes" and not for all couples, causes that you've to postpone the intimate life. Although some may be surprised when I say that, it is also true that there are couples who end up displeased by menstruation. There are people who have a hard time having to put up with the desire (to have sex).

For some the solution is to use a condom and with that they close the chapter perfectly. Here free will is definitely applicable.

Interviewing many people, I have noticed that couples do not talk much about the subject. When the time comes or accept it or seek other alternatives of satisfaction.

Menstruation is a topic where hygiene, cultural, religious and educational values of the family are intertwined. All the factors contribute to the development of a specific perception on the matter, and even, the establishment of an attitude and certain behaviors.

Many times, people perceive menstruation as something dirty, even unpleasant and very intimate, which means that during that period sex is not practiced.

The most frequent complaint of men about this period of menstruation is the bad character of the woman, which causes conflicts in the couple and especially dislikes. There are few who are saved from this.

Men are not aware of or keep track of when their partner will have menstruation again. There is when it falls on the weekend! This causes faces of disgust, often mutual.

We have advised many mothers that proper preparation of their daughters is important, in relation to menstruation. We know that there are mothers who only inform their daughters that the bleeding will be every month and that they now have knowing that they are exposed to having a pregnancy if they decide to have sex. Although these are undeniable truths, it does not point out that it is a life event that should represent happiness, despite the inconveniences of cleanliness and care that it requires, since menstruation lets them know that they will one day be mothers.

There are girls that menstruation appears at very early ages. I think you could tell them that your uterus is preparing for a party, in which " little balloons full of blood" await the visit of a sperm, which will cause fertilization and pregnancy. When no sperm arrives, the party ends and the balloons break, and the bleeding they have occurs.

Later this process is repeated every certain number of weeks until a pregnancy appears where this process is stopped. The cycle will appear later.

Women enjoy this privilege, characterized by being those who guarantee the continuity of human beings for centuries. Wonderful! Right?

That's why the woman's belly is something extraordinary. Menstruation represents the perpetuation of the species. This biological process is linked to the Force of Pleasure, but it has ties with the Force of Responsibility and with the Force of Love when you've sought a family out of love.

11- IS THE RELATION TO BE CONTINUED OR NOT TO CONTINUE?

Many have been caught in the next question, should I continue this relationship or not?

Not everything in love is easy, nor does it have a rational explanation, we have already said.

Not for pleasure until the Brain has two hemispheres whose functions are different, although complementary. Love seems to "live hidden" in the right hemisphere, which is responsible for emotions, fantasies, states of happiness, passion and suffering. But the interesting thing is that passion is not forever in most cases.

What keeps the motivation alive is another brain structure, the Accumbens Nucleus. If one of those involved in the love relationship, is often hyperactivity, he or she may need constant and immediate reinforcement of affection, attention and more. Otherwise, the motivation that feeds the illusion and passion may decay earlier than expected in these people.

There are authors who claim that the Accumbens is responsible for our reactions to a separation or loss.

Everything seems to indicate that the Brain has well distributed its responsibilities. It seems that love is more related to the Brain than to the Heart.

Everything is not there. At the Albert Einstein College of Medicine in New York he has been working on the search for the circuit of love. They have isolated the following regions and given them very unromantic names: Ventral Tegmental Area (ATV), Accumbens Nucleus, Pale Ventral and Dorsal Raphe Nucleus.

The interesting thing is that ATV is illuminated in studies with magnetic resonance when the person is in love. When love has a long history, the Pale Ventral and Dorsal Nucleus of the Raphe also light up.

With the previous preamble, it is easier to continue. I ask you to carefully analyze the following situation that happens every day in real life. It happens that two people begin to feel an attraction that suffocates, that covers their thinking and distracts them, that makes them wonder if it is normal to feel this way, that reason does not want to work, that they think it should not be, but they want see each other and talk and hug.

They recognize that when they are together, the chest is overwhelmed with so many beats and fear invade them. Both have a stable life as a couple. How could this have happened to them?

Love does not ask permission to present itself. Love does it when it seems best. It is a force that stops for a while to be repressed, but in that moment, it reveals itself and asks that its demands be satisfied. Let us not forget that it belongs to the reign of survival, conservation and perpetuity of the human species. If the human being did not mate and copulate, there would be no new generations that would continue the story.

Therefore, it is not surprising that it is imposed against principles, rules, norms and commitments. Generally, it arises when you find someone who is perceived as the person who catches your heart. If so, it is because we are living a relationship with another person who is incomplete in some aspect. Something missing. It is not that the other person is not good, it is that it does not completely satisfy the soul and the desire.

What is happening is a great element to reach a diagnosis. We are dissatisfied! That's why we are attracted to another person, there's no doubt about it.

What this conclusion suggests is that we seek to be sure that the passion we are feeling is lasting and convenient. They are two different things.

To know that it could be durable several ingredients are necessary.

One of them is that the passion is maintained over time. May the feelings awakened prove to be consistent and capable of fighting against all odds. That tastes are explored calmly and in different scenarios, the ability to do different things, although complementary for both, without letting it pass well and knowing that it can make the other feel good and even happy.

You've to let mature this "forbidden" relationship. Here come the spiritual risks and of all kinds. Because if the decision is made to make sure that the passion is true, besides sharing time talking and going out at times, both will wonder if they would feel satisfied in the bed.

This is a difficult, but decisive test to know if the magic of love is real or illusory.

Let's say that it grows and consolidates, that what is shared points out that passion is true. Now, it remains to be defined if it is convenient.

How much do you put yourself at risk?

Let's not forget that he was born unexpectedly and spontaneously.

It is also true that it was decided not to abandon this gift of life.

The decision was made despite its risks, to know its intensity and durability. We deliver everything without fear. But the responsibility remains with others and with oneself. Affecting others and changing their lives and their own is a delicate task.

Now come the determinations.

1- Or research is avoided from the beginning, avoiding the risks involved. Which means that you will not know if it was real or not. But wounds and possible laments were avoided.

2 - Or become aware that the passion felt is a sign that our soul is thirsty. That sooner or later will complain again.

3- That we are dissatisfied and that we should seek a remedy for what happens to us.

Difficult, right?

12- THERE IS NOT ALWAYS A SECOND OPPORTUNITY.

Not always in life do the same opportunities appear twice. For undecided, for being perfectionists, for believing that we have more time and because we think that we should not rush, or for what others will say of our actions, or for that EGO, that we both spoil and help him to have a high sense of unnecessary and sterile pride, that lets escape what is perhaps and will be, our only chance. At any age this situation can occur. If we are not prepared, we lose it and then regrets come.

Routines are the daily shadows that give life to the scenario of cities and towns. Many people fill the cellars of the cities without their wine being aged. They have walked through life repeating what others do, looking for stability and security, but they are not full or satisfied.

Many have asked themselves, why is life being born and dying? It's clear that between one point and another, many things happen. For others, they question it in a different way, what is my mission and that of everyone in life?

There are also other questions, such as: What are we born for? Where do we go when we die?

Finally, we know that there is an end. But before it arrives, it is hard for us to think and accept that we've to make sacrifices, tolerate pain and make changes. Although Love regulates Life, let us not forget that Fear plays a great role in the history of every person.

Many are not successful in business, because they do not take risks. The same happens in Love. Not everyone ends their lives, living in a Castle of Happiness.

"Someone is happy, who, after the years, can see his own Castle, made of bricks of beautiful memories, painted with exceptional Emotions and Furnished with his dreams made Reality." PJ

Everything depends, for what we live and what we dedicate ourselves in life.

The hurtful phrases, the screams, the unpleasant adjectives cannot express the tenderness of the affection.

In all the scenarios that this happens the victims do not stop feeling that they exclude it. The abuser, who feels power to mistreat and expects to be tolerated and who is often tolerated for good weather, does not stop making the victim feel that he can leave, that it is not important in his life. What a clearer way to say to another person: "you do not belong to the special circle of life, of my loved ones, of those I need and love"

In all the scenarios that this happens the victims do not stop feeling that they exclude it. The abuser, who feels power to mistreat and expects to be tolerated and who is often tolerated for good weather, does not stop making the victim feel that he can leave, that it is not important in his life. What a clearer way to tell another person: "you do not belong to the special circle of my life, of my loved ones, of those I need and love"

I hope you have been able to show that we are talking about love and its multiple links with other forces and events in life.

13- I REMOVED THE SOMBREO.

Yes, to those who after reading the book decide not to reject those who think differently, those who make mistakes and repent, those who are physically or mentally different, those who have preferences that are not ours, to whom the circumstances of life deprived them of the necessary education in our times, adults who do not know the technology of smartphones or computers, those who are poor, the vagabonds of those who almost we never know their history, women that to survive they have had to sacrifice their dignity and their bodies, to which arrogance characterizes them for having more than others, for those who feel envy, because envy is the desire to have what others have, like jealousy is the fear of being taken away from what we think belongs to us and we do not want to share.

It is difficult to achieve all that, but not impossible. The human miseries have always existed, fighting against them allows us to have peace and give it to others, since to avoid rejecting others, it makes us able to contribute to one of the important columns of Love, not being affected when we interact with other people .

It is no less true that there are those who deserve our rejection and exclusion from our lives. No rule without exception. Everyone has their reasons.

In the Security-Protection column, Respect, Tolerance and Understanding are included. Regarding Respect, its violation is frequent. We see it when we are driving. Some people do not put the indicators that they are going to turn on right and it takes us by surprise.

Other people make a sudden turn and come forward without anticipating the consequences. Of course. They are sure that if we hit them from behind, we would be the culprits and not them.

There are homes that teenagers enter and do not greet those present, leaving adults in an embarrassing situation many times. It is not uncommon for many of us to raise our voices when we get upset. It is not uncommon for us to interrupt others while they are talking, without having the patience to wait our turn or ask permission to be allowed to speak.

These examples and many more than sure comes to your head happen and tell us how much we still must work to achieve a positive change in our lives.

Everything said, of course, affects the Force of Love and that is why we are as we are. I would take my hat off if there are people who do not make these mistakes.

Patience does not go hand in hand with tolerance. There are things that cannot be tolerated, because they become offensive. We can learn to wait at certain times, but we cannot tolerate certain disrespectful behaviors in social or family life. When we offend ourselves with someone, that person can take it as if we are excluding them from our circle, that we do not accept them, and everything ends in distance and separation. What Force of Live intervened? After reading the book there is no doubt, that they know the answer.

Now it only remains to practice. The tools and knowledge that has already been provided.

AKNOWLEDGEMENT

Advances in Parapsychological Research. Stantley Kripper, Adam Rock, Julie Beischel, Harris L Friedman and Chery L Fracasso. Publisher: Jefferson, NC, USA. 2013.

Biofeedback. A Practitioner's Guide. Second Edition. Mark S. Schwartz and Associates. Guilford Press. New York, London 1995.

Como agua para chocolate – Laura Esquivel. Anchor Brooks. Random House Inc. New York. Publicado en México Planetas. 1989.

Frank S. Caprio. El Hombre Sexualmente Adecuado. Editorial Constancia, S. A. México, 1957.

Floyd E. Bloom, M. Flint Beal, David J. Kupfer. The Dana guide to Brain Health. The Free Press, New York 2003

Geral Corey. Case Approach to Counseling and Psychotherapy.Brooks/ Cole Publishing Company, California, 1991.

Jeffery K Zeig. The Evolution of Psychotherapy. The Third Conference. Brunner/ Marzel, Publishres. New York, 1995.

José Martí. Obras Completas Tomo 21. Editorial Ciencias Sociales. La Habana, Cuba, 1975.

El Amor Regula la Vida. ISBN 978-0-9856883-0-1.

Siegfried Schnabl. El Hombre y la Mujer en la intimidad. Editorial Científico Técnica, Habana, Cuba, 1978.

Spencer A Rathus, Jefrey S. Nevid, Lois Fichner-Rathus. Huaman Sexuality in the World of Diversity. Third Edition. Allyn and Bacon. A Viacom Company, MA, 1993.

The Dana Guide to Brain Health. Floyd E. Bloom, M.D., M. Flint Beal, M.D., David J. Kuffer, M.D. The Dana Press. New York. NY. 2003.